MAKING ·MASKS·

FOR CHILDREN

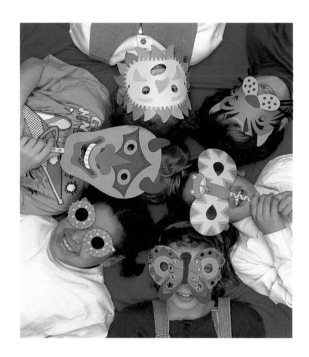

GILLIAN CHAPMAN · PAM ROBSON

MACDONALD YOUNG BOOKS

A Chinese dragon's in the street
And dancing on its Chinese feet
With fearsome head and golden scale
And twisting its ferocious tail.
Its bulging eyes are blazing red
While smoke is puffing from its head
And well you nervously might ask
What lies behind the fearful mask.

from *Dragon Dance* by Max Fatchen

This book was prepared for
Macdonald Young Books Ltd
by Globe Education
Nantwich, Cheshire

Visualisation and design:
Gillian Chapman
Photography:
Rupert Horrox

Special thanks to Brantwood
Design Services for extra help
with the model making and to
Beric Tempest Ltd for their help
with the cover and page headings

Additional photographs:
Martyn Chillmaid, title page
Werner Forman, pages 4 and 5
Telegraph Colour Library/John
Lander, page 21

First published in 1995
by Macdonald Young Books Ltd
Campus 400, Maylands Avenue
Hemel Hempstead, Herts HP2 7EZ

Text © 1995 Gillian Chapman
and Pam Robson
Illustration © Gillian Chapman

A catalogue record for
this book is available from
the British Library

ISBN 0 7500 1769 4

Printed in Portugal.

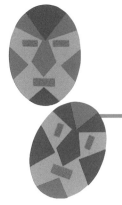

CONTENTS

WHY MASKS?

Ancient people wore masks during rituals and ceremonies in the belief that the masks changed them into spirits, animals, devils or even gods. Over the centuries, masks have been used to express human beliefs and customs. The link with magic and superstition continues into modern times with celebrations such as Hallowe'en. The difference today is that people enjoy such events because they are fun.

Mask Styles

A mask can hide part of the face or the whole face. It can even cover the whole head. It may be a copy of a face or be a simple covering worn for protection. The word mask is derived from masque or masquerade. A masque was a form of entertainment popular in England during the 17th century.

This mask was made by the Tlingit Indians of North America. It represents the face of an old woman's spirit.

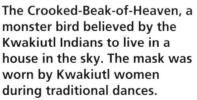

The Crooked-Beak-of-Heaven, a monster bird believed by the Kwakiutl Indians to live in a house in the sky. The mask was worn by Kwakiutl women during traditional dances.

Changing Faces

To cover your face or head with a mask is to transform yourself. Suddenly you can become anonymous, no-one knows who you are.

For people who are shy, it is a chance to behave in a different way. It is a chance to lose inhibitions. This can be fun at parties or celebrations. There are those who wish to hide for the wrong reasons. Thieves and burglars, for example, cover their faces so witnesses cannot identify them.

Protecting Faces

The face is the most vulnerable part of the body. It needs protection during dangerous activities. In the later Middle Ages when a knight wore armour, his helmet had a hinged visor to protect his face. There were slits for the eyes. Modern baseball caps also have a peak or visor that keeps the sun out of the wearer's eyes.

Fashionable Faces

In the 17th century, ladies often wore an oval mask or vizard when going to the theatre. A full-face vizard gave protection against the weather and was held in place by a bead fastened inside the mask and held between the teeth. Usually these masks were more to do with fashion than with protection.

Many Personalities

Person comes from a Latin word, 'persona', meaning mask. In Ancient Greece, actors wore masks on stage. Not only could they disguise their own personalities, but they could show a variety of others. The same person could play many parts. The look on someone's face is sometimes known as their phizog. In the theatre the word phizog means a mask that represents a certain personality. Masks allow freedom of expression and they can help people communicate. There are modern theatre groups that use mime, relying upon masks and movements as forms of expression.

A tortoiseshell mask from New Ireland in the Pacific Ocean.

MASQUES AND DISGUISES

Eye masks were traditionally worn by people taking part in fancy dress parties known as masquerades. The masks were often very imaginative and it was fun to try to recognise the people underneath. Eye masks were also once worn by infamous characters who wished to disguise themselves. Each country has its own villains. Notorious highwaymen, like Dick Turpin, robbed travellers and yet have become legends.

Party Masks

Simple eye masks are easy to make and great fun to wear at parties. Thin flexible card is an ideal material to use. Be careful not to use heavy materials for decoration.

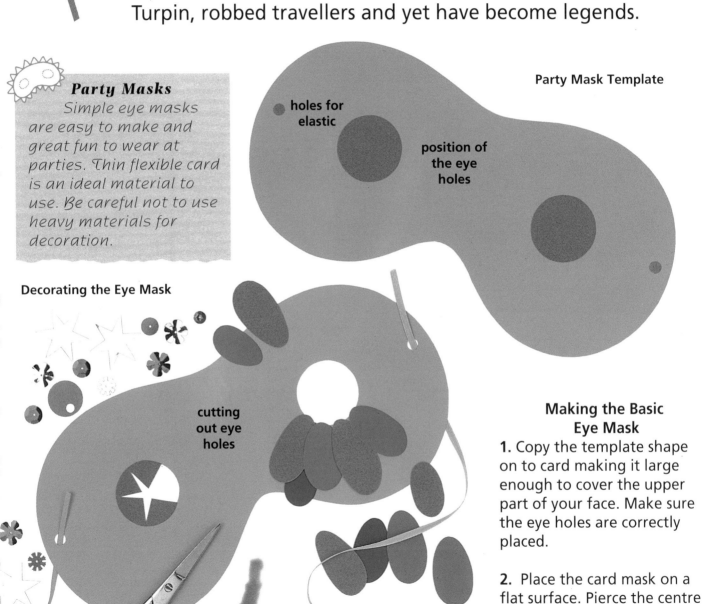

Party Mask Template

holes for elastic

position of the eye holes

Decorating the Eye Mask

cutting out eye holes

Making the Basic Eye Mask

1. Copy the template shape on to card making it large enough to cover the upper part of your face. Make sure the eye holes are correctly placed.

2. Place the card mask on a flat surface. Pierce the centre of each eyehole with a sharp pencil point. Trim away the extra card with small scissors.

Decorating the Eye Mask

1. Decorate the mask. Use paint, or glue on scraps of coloured paper and fabric. Try lightweight materials such as feathers and pipe cleaners. Add extra sparkle with glitter, sequins and coloured foil. If the mask is to be part of a fancy dress costume, decorate it to suit the character.

2. You could attach small pieces of coloured netting to the back of the mask so they veil the eye holes.

3. Make small holes at each side of the mask through which to thread elastic or ribbon. It will need to to be long enough to stretch around the back of your head but tight enough to hold the mask in place.

4. You could tape the mask to a stick and hold it in front of your face.

Party Masks

don't forget to decorate the stick

Decorated Sunglasses

Dark Disguises

Famous people who want to go unnoticed sometimes wear dark glasses.

Old sunglasses are ready-made frames for eye masks. By glueing coloured paper or fabric shapes to the plastic frame and decorating them with different materials, they can look very dramatic.

ACTORS AND PERFORMERS

Greek theatres were in the open air and so huge that the actors wore masks to allow the audience to recognise each of the characters. Specially-shaped mouthpieces made the sounds louder so the audience could hear their words. In Japan 600 years ago, Noh theatre used painted wooden masks. Today, circus clowns wear thick make-up to create funny faces.

Making a Clown Mask

1. Mark out the position of the eyes, the nose and the mouth on a paper plate.

2. Carefully cut the holes for the eyes. Attach a ping-pong ball for the nose.

3. Decorate the mask with paints or felt pens. You could also use paper, fabric or feathers.

4. Attach elastic to fit round the back of your head, or support the mask on a stick.

Clown Make-Up
Each clown has their own special style of face painting and no clown copies another. You could try copying a clown face from an information book or you could invent a design of your own.

Paper Plate Clown Masks with Traditional Clown Faces

Flat Sun Mask

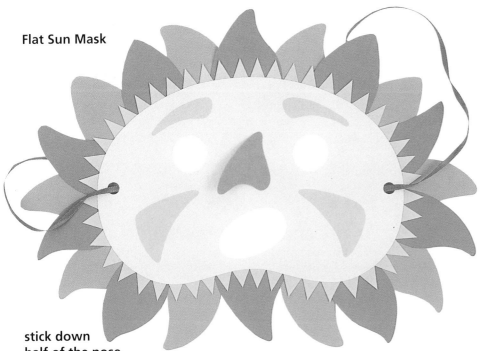

stick down
half of the nose
and fold the other half out

Making a Flat Mask

1. First sketch your ideas out on paper and then transfer them to card. The larger the mask, the thicker the card needs to be.

2. Cut out the mask and make holes for the eyes and mouth.

3. Attach elastic to hold the mask to your head or use a stick for support.

Drama
A comedy needs happy faces and a tragedy needs the opposite. If rapid changes of mood are required, the actors can wear reversible masks with one happy face and one sad face.

Making a Reversible Mask

1. First sketch your ideas out on paper. You need two different faces with the same outline.

2. Cut two identical shaped pieces of card. Make eye and mouth holes through both pieces of card.

3. Transfer your designs and glue the two pieces back-to-back with a stick between for support.

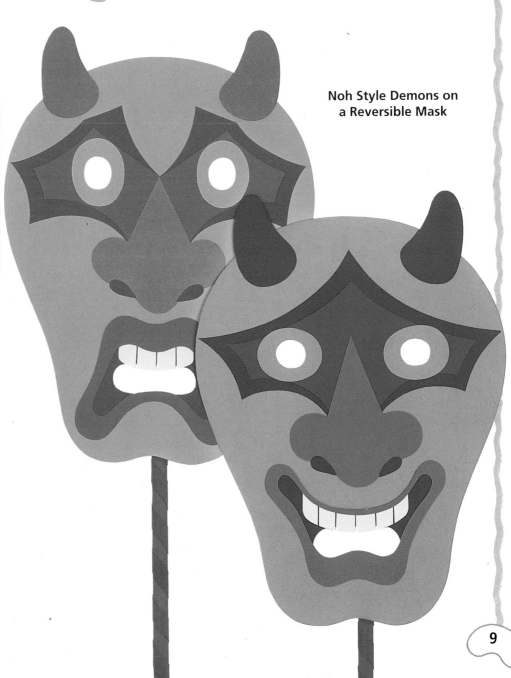

Noh Style Demons on a Reversible Mask

9

SOLDIERS AND CIVILIANS

Battles in the Middle Ages depended on hand to hand combat. Knights needed protection against sword thrusts and axe blows. Metal suits of armour were topped with helmets that reached down to the shoulders. Minstrels wandered from place to place entertaining villagers with songs and spreading news of distant events like battles. They often wore colourful and distinctive costumes.

Making a Paper Bag Hood

1. Lay the bag flat and tuck in the bottom corners as shown in the diagram.

2. Draw the hood outline on the bag.

3. Cut out the face piece and the edge pattern.

4. Paint a design on the hood.

5. Decorate it with coloured paper or felt shapes.

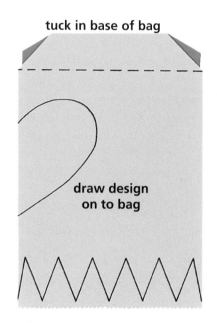

tuck in base of bag

draw design on to bag

Shaping the Bag and Positioning the Design

Minstrel's Decorative Hood

Paper Bag Hoods
A decorative hood or helmet can easily be made from a strong paper bag. Use a heavy duty bag, large enough to fit over your head.
Do not put a plastic bag over your head.

A Knight's Helmet

This was the most important part of his armour. Some designs reached down to the shoulders. Can you imagine wearing a heavy metal helmet? It must have been very difficult to see.

Design A

Design B

Making a Knight's Helmet

1. Cut out the helmet shape from the paper bag.

2. Design A has the eye holes cut out from the front of the bag.

3. Design B is made in the same way as the hood but has a card visor attached with paper fasteners.

4. Glue coiled lengths of string on to the helmet to create a raised pattern.

5. Paint the helmet with metallic poster paint.

6. Glue on the small circles from a hole punch to look like metal rivets.

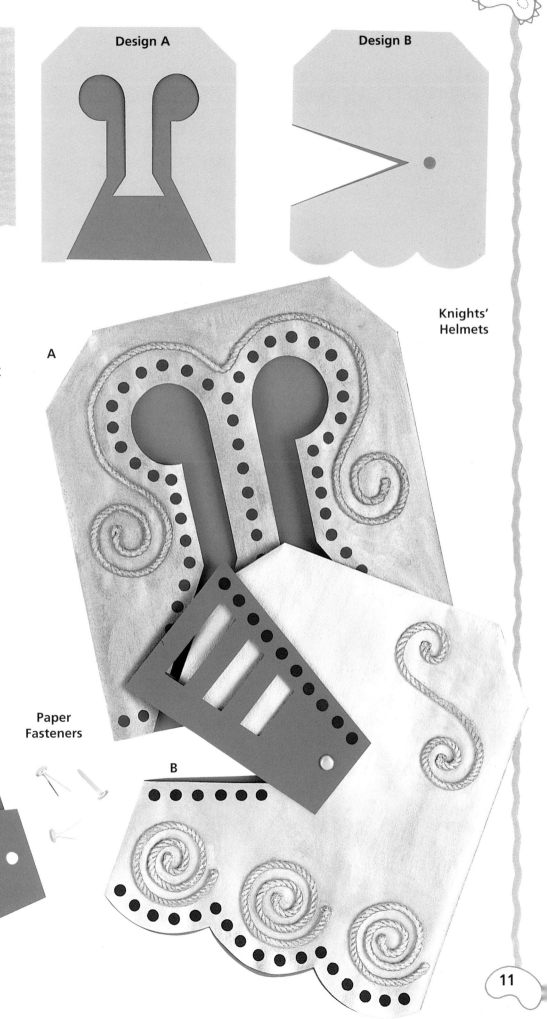

Knights' Helmets

A

Paper Fasteners

B

Card Visor

11

FESTIVAL MASKS

A festival is an organised celebration and most festivals have their origins in the distant past. They usually have traditional customs and costumes. In Java and Bali, there is a strong tradition of masked dance. Dancers wear painted wooden masks and extravagant costumes. In New Guinea, dancers wear conical masks that enclose the head completely. They extend below the waist and have armholes in the sides.

Measuring Card for Cylindrical Masks

1. Find card that is flexible enough to bend into shape but strong enough to support any decoration.

2. Measure out a rectangle 40 cm x 60 cm and cut out as shown in diagram A.

3. Bend round into a cylinder and fasten lightly with masking tape.

Measuring Card for Conical Masks

1. Again find flexible but strong card.

2. Draw a quarter of a circle with a radius of 60 cm as shown in diagram B. There should be a right angle at the centre of the circle.

3. Bend round into a cone and fasten lightly with a paper-clip or masking tape.

Diagram A

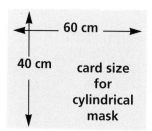

60 cm
40 cm
card size for cylindrical mask

Diagram B

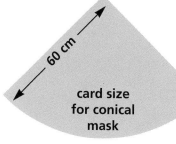

60 cm
card size for conical mask

tape

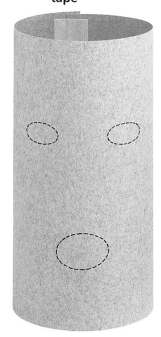

tape or clip temporarily in place

clip

cut out nose and ear flaps when mask is open flat

Making Festival Masks

1. Make either a cylindrical or a conical mask shape.

2. Put it on and ask a friend to help you mark the position of the eye and mouth holes with a pencil.

3. Open up the mask. It will be easier to cut out the eye and mouth holes neatly if the card is flat.

4. Roll the mask back into shape and use strong adhesive tape to hold it together.

5. Decorate your mask. Use extra coloured shapes for features and use different materials to make interesting textures. All your collage materials must be glued firmly to the mask to keep them secure.

Practical Ideas

If you are making a large mask for a particular purpose think your ideas through before you begin. Will you be acting or dancing in the mask? Can you see where you are going and move freely?

It must be secure and comfortable to wear especially if you will be wearing it for a long time.

look at photographs of traditional masks for ideas for your festival masks

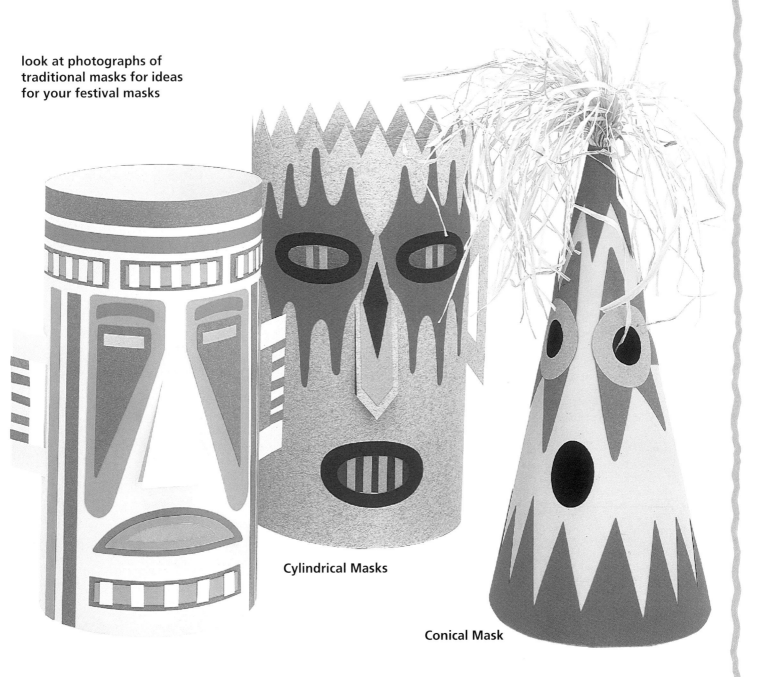

Cylindrical Masks

Conical Mask

CARNIVAL MASKS

Carnival was once a festival linked to Christian celebrations in the week before the beginning of Lent. It was often known as Mardi Gras. Venice in Italy had a carnival season that lasted from January until Lent. Revellers wore masks of many patterns and colours. There were animal heads and monsters as well as realistic masks. Hand-held masks were popular. Venice had many skilled mask-makers.

Making Carnival Masks

1. Make a simple eye mask shape from card (see page 6). Folding the mask in half may help the fit.

2. Build up fur or feather textures by overlapping pieces of coloured paper or fabric.

3. A beak can be made from coloured paper. Cut out a beak shape, as shown below.

4. Fold the beak and glue it to the mask.

5. Cut out feather shapes and stick over the glue flaps so they are hidden.

6. Paper ears and plumes can be attached to the back of the mask.

7. Place coloured netting over the eye holes to make a more mysterious disguise.

8. Use sequins, feathers and glitter to add glamour.

Making the Basic Mask

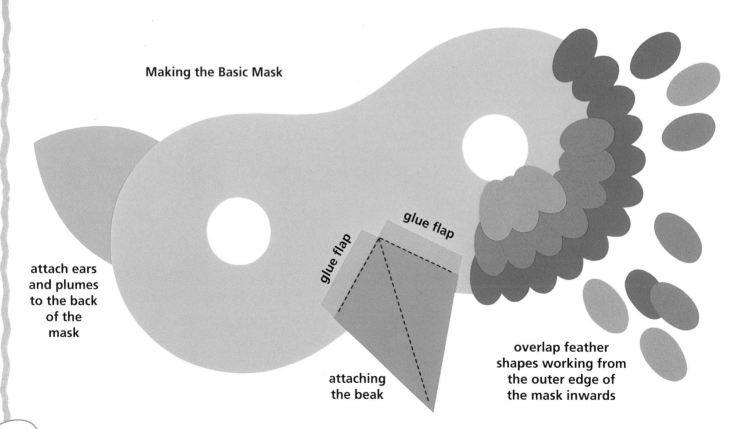

attach ears and plumes to the back of the mask

glue flap

glue flap

attaching the beak

overlap feather shapes working from the outer edge of the mask inwards

Supporting the Mask

1. Because these masks can be large and top heavy, you need to make a card framework that sits on top of your head.

2. Measure your head first and cut the strips to size.

3. Glue or tape the strips firmly to the back of the mask as shown here.

Supporting the Mask

glue strips to back of mask

Adding Final Touches

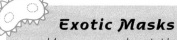

Exotic Masks

You can adapt this method of making masks to make any creature or bird mask. There is plenty of scope for making very exotic and imaginative masks to complement a fancy dress costume.

ANCIENT MASKS

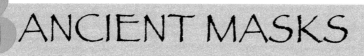

The Iroquois Indians made sun masks from corn husks, believing that they represented the spirit of the corn. Other ancient tribes believed that the wearer of a wooden mask would receive some of the power of the original tree. Many different natural materials have been used throughout time to decorate masks – shells, feathers, bones, fibres, even fish scales and spiders' webs.

Making Masks from Natural Materials

1. First make a collection of interesting natural materials and then plan out your design on paper to make best use of them.

2. Make a card base for your mask. It can be any size or shape.

3. Draw your design on to the card base and position the eye and mouth holes. Cut them out neatly.

4. Decide how you will support the mask. A heavy mask may be better on a stick. A lighter mask could be fixed with elastic round the back of your head.

5. Using a strong water-based adhesive, cover the card base with textures. String and raffia can be coiled into shapes around the eyes and mouth, as shown here.

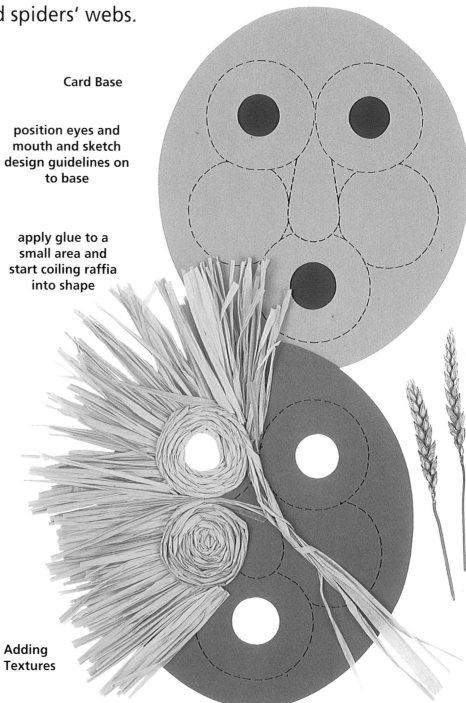

Card Base

position eyes and mouth and sketch design guidelines on to base

apply glue to a small area and start coiling raffia into shape

Adding Textures

16

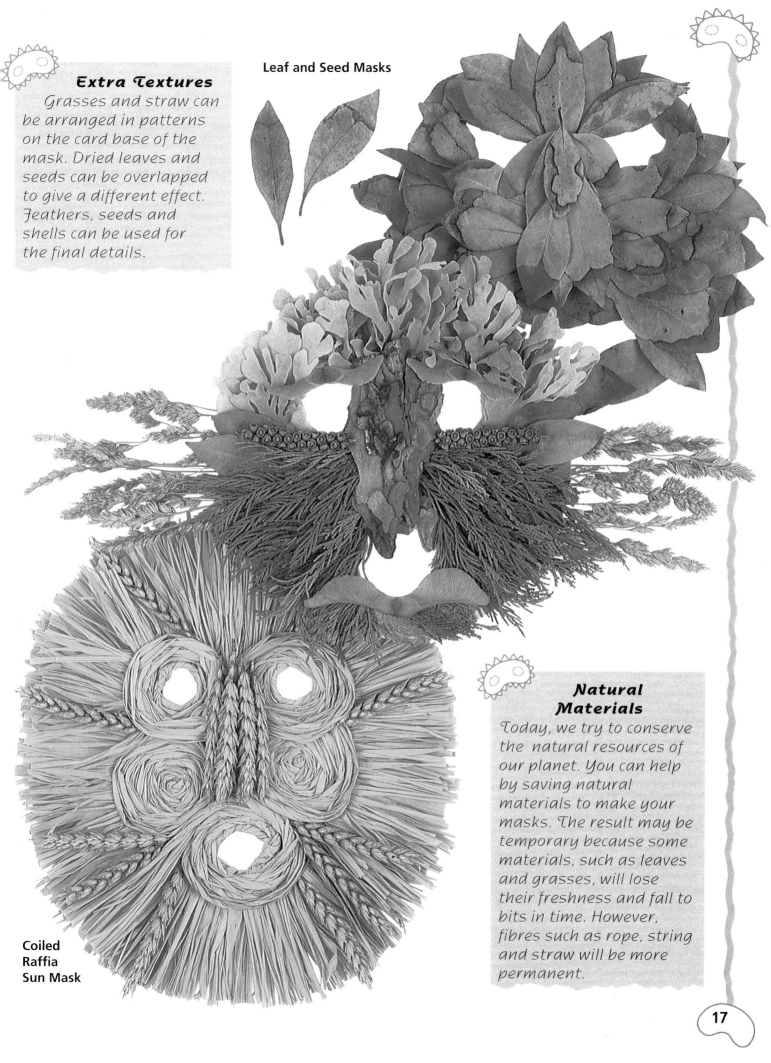

Extra Textures

Grasses and straw can be arranged in patterns on the card base of the mask. Dried leaves and seeds can be overlapped to give a different effect. Feathers, seeds and shells can be used for the final details.

Leaf and Seed Masks

Natural Materials

Today, we try to conserve the natural resources of our planet. You can help by saving natural materials to make your masks. The result may be temporary because some materials, such as leaves and grasses, will lose their freshness and fall to bits in time. However, fibres such as rope, string and straw will be more permanent.

Coiled Raffia Sun Mask

MODERN MASKS

Artists like Picasso were inspired by the craftwork of ancient civilisations. The distinctive style of traditional African masks can be seen in some of their work. In Australia, modern artists recycle plastic to create artefacts like masks in the traditional style. In the islands of the Torres Straits, masks were once made from turtleshell, now many are made from discarded plastic.

Making a Junk Collection
Collect cardboard packets and boxes that would otherwise be thrown away, also fabric, foil and old magazines. Save discarded plastic, but make sure all bottles and containers are completely clean. Foil is easy to cut and emboss but the edges can be sharp.

Foil Mask

'Picasso' Collage Mask

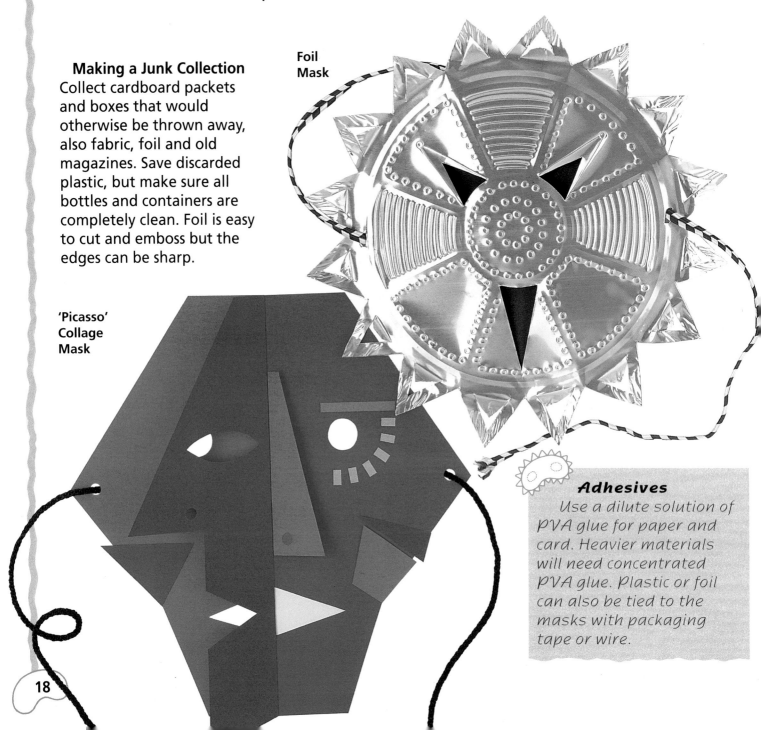

Adhesives
Use a dilute solution of PVA glue for paper and card. Heavier materials will need concentrated PVA glue. Plastic or foil can also be tied to the masks with packaging tape or wire.

Recycling

Discarded plastic objects create a major problem in the world because most cannot be recycled or destroyed. To use plastic to create a work of art is to put to good use what would otherwise be an environmental problem.

Use coloured Cellophane for eyes. When you use plastic film or bubble wrap to make a mask always stick it on to a card backing. **Make sure it doesn't cover your mouth and nose.**

Mosaic Mask with Lids and Bottle Tops

Making Modern Masks

1. Work out your design for your mask starting with a simple card base. Think about the materials you have in your junk collection so you can make best use of them.

2. Cut out the card base and transfer your design on to it.

3. Cut holes for the mouth and the eyes.

4. Add decoration to the mask building up the layers of your design.

5. Support the mask with a stick or elastic to go round your head.

**Curly
Tape
Mask**

19

MASKS AND MAKE-UP

People across the world paint their faces to change the way they look, especially actors in plays and films. In Japan, Kabuki theatre players follow ancient rituals and traditions. Certain colours and designs belong to specific characters. In Mabuiag in the Torres Strait, the Rainmaker would paint himself white in front and black behind, symbolic of rain clouds. He would also wear a head-dress and a hideous mask.

Painted Faces

A papier mâché balloon mask makes a good base on which to paint a face. Papier mâché is very strong and the painted face can be used many times.

Making a Balloon Mask Base

1. Blow up a balloon to the size of your head. Smear the balloon with a generous coating of petroleum jelly.

2. Tear up newspaper and cover the balloon with the pieces, glueing them down with diluted PVA adhesive.

3. You will need about 6 layers of paper. Use different coloured paper so you can tell the layers apart. Leave to dry completely. This takes about 3 days.

4. Pop the balloon and cut the papier mâché shape into two oval halves.

Layers of Newspaper Glued on to Balloon Mould

Cutting the Dried Shape in Half to Make Two Mask Bases

Painting the Mask

1. Look through information books about traditional face painting and choose a design. We have used a Kabuki face to paint in our example here.

2. Plan your face design and sketch it in pencil on to the mask base.

3. Make sure the eye and mouth holes will match up with yours and carefully cut the holes with a craft knife.

4. Use poster paints to paint the main part of the face white and colour in the detail following your design.

5. Make holes in the sides and thread elastic through.

Masks with 'Kabuki' Painted Faces

Reference Picture of Kabuki Face

Outline of Kabuki Design Sketched on to the Mask Base

Further Ideas

You could make a half mask to cover just the upper part of your face by cutting away the lower half of the mask shape. The exposed half of your face could be painted with face paints to match the mask. Papier mâché masks are very light and can be supported by elastic.

21

MAGICAL MASKS

In many ancient cultures, the wearing of a mask bestows great powers on the wearer. In Nigeria, the Ekoi tribe make large helmet-shaped wooden masks. These masks usually have three faces. Each face looks in a different direction showing that the spirit of the mask can look both into the past and into the future and as a result knows everything. The Fang tribe make helmet masks with as many as six faces.

Making the Base for a Mask with Many Faces

1. You will need a cardboard box that will fit over your head and rest on your shoulders.

2. Choose whether your mask is to have Design A or Design B. Design A makes use of the edge of the box and has two faces. Design B has a different face on each of the four sides.

3. Decide how many faces your mask is to have and sketch them on to the box.

4. Make sure that the eye and mouth holes are in the right place for your face. You may need a friend to help you.

Design A
use the edge of the box to form the nose or beak; cut out mouth and eye holes

Design B
use the sides of the box for each face; position the eye and mouth holes on each size

A. Two-faced Parrot Mask

Powerful Masks
Near the Arctic Circle the weather is always cold and few trees grow. At a time when the Inuit relied entirely on nature to live in this cold climate, they believed that all natural things contained spirits. Wood was precious and to capture its spirit, they held ceremonies involving wooden animal masks.

In countries in Africa, masks represented the spirits of dead ancestors.

B. Multi-faced Mask

Decorating a Mask with Many Faces

1. Each face can be different. The wearer could play several roles at the same time. Think about the moods and expressions that you want to show.

2. Look at other masks in this book for ideas for showing the features and adding decoration to the final mask.

3. Use different collage materials and textures to create a range of different effects.

4. Don't forget to decorate the top of the box.

SHAPING FACES

Inspiration for the design of elaborate masks can be found in cultures all over the world. Totem poles in Polynesia and North America have carvings of spirit faces, part human, part animal. Peoples of America and Africa have festivals in which the dancers wear huge wooden masks carved with animal and human figures. In Asia, dance masks are traditionally made from papier mâché.

Making the Base for a Moulded Mask

1. You will need either modelling clay or Plasticine. Both are ideal materials for making a mould.

2. Make a life size sketch of your mask on paper.

3. Take enough modelling material to make the face shape and place it on a board.

4. Following your design, mould the material to the shape of the face and then add the features.

5. If you make a mistake, you can easily remould the features. Make them larger than life because covering them with papier mâché will fill and flatten them

6. Coat the mould with plenty of petroleum jelly.

Sketch of Mask Design

Making the Mould

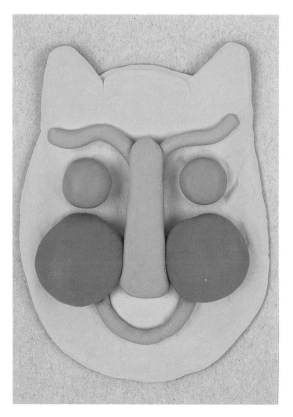

Making and Decorating the Mask

1. Cover your mould with layers of papier mâché as described on page 20.

2. Carefully remove the mask from the clay mould and clean the excess petroleum jelly from the back of the mask.

3. Sketch your original design on to the front of the mask.

4. Cut holes for the eyes, the nose, and mouth using a craft knife. Make sure they line up with the wearer's eyes, nose and mouth.

5. Paint the mask with poster paints and when the paint is dry, give it a coat of varnish to protect and strengthen it.

6. Masks made of papier mâché are very light and can be attached to the head with elastic.

make small holes in the cheeks and add pipe cleaner whiskers

sketch features on to the paper mask base and cut out the eyes and mouth

'Asian' style Dance Mask

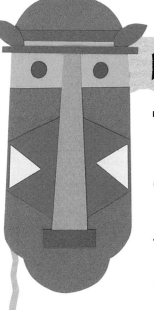

MASKS WITH MOVING PARTS

The Kwakiutl Indians of North America had large, dramatic transformation masks. They were believed to change the dancer into another spirit. A raven mask opens to show a human descendant and a thunderbird mask flaps its wings. Tlingit masks, also from North America, have articulated jaws and moving eye lids. In Mexico, dancers celebrating the Day of the Dead perform in skull masks with moving jaws.

Making Mexican Skull Masks

1. Sketch out your design for the skull mask the right size to fit your head.

2. Make a papier mâché mask base using either the balloon method on page 20 or the mould method on page 24.

3. Cut eye and nose holes in the mask using a craft knife.

4. Make the bottom jaw from card as shown here. It needs to be the right size to fit your mask.

5. Attach the jaw to the skull with paper fasteners. Fix a stick to the inside of the jaw so that it can be opened and closed.

6. Attach elastic to the skull to fit round your head.

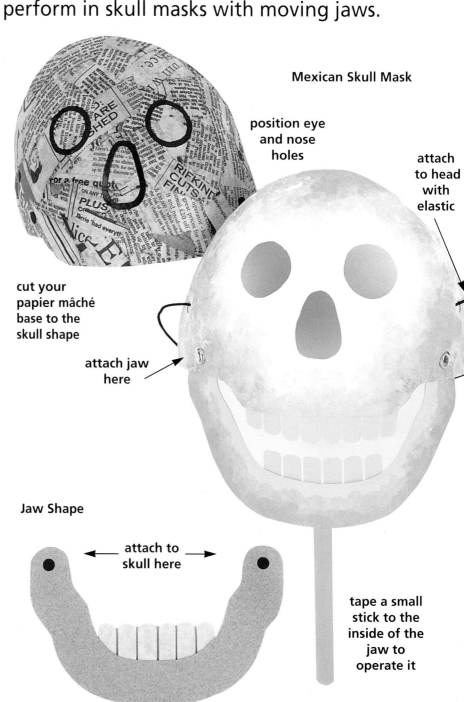

cut your papier mâché base to the skull shape

position eye and nose holes

Mexican Skull Mask

attach to head with elastic

attach jaw here

Jaw Shape

← attach to skull here →

tape a small stick to the inside of the jaw to operate it

26

Making a Transformation Mask

1. First make a papier mâché mask base using the balloon method on page 20.

2. Sketch a face on to the mask base. Cut out eye and mouth holes using a craft knife.

3. Cut two beak shapes from card as shown in the diagram.

4. Make 4 small holes in each beak flap and at each side of the mask, making sure they line up. These are the sewing holes.

5. Make holes A, B and C in the mask and beaks. These are the holes for the strings.

6. Paint the mask using poster paints. Try to follow the traditional designs as closely as possible.

7. Thread a long length of string through one side of the mask at a time, as shown. Tie together the two strings that thread through holes A. Then tie together the strings from holes C.

8. Support the mask on a stick. Thread the pairs of strings through small eyelets screwed into the stick. Pull the strings to open and close the beak.

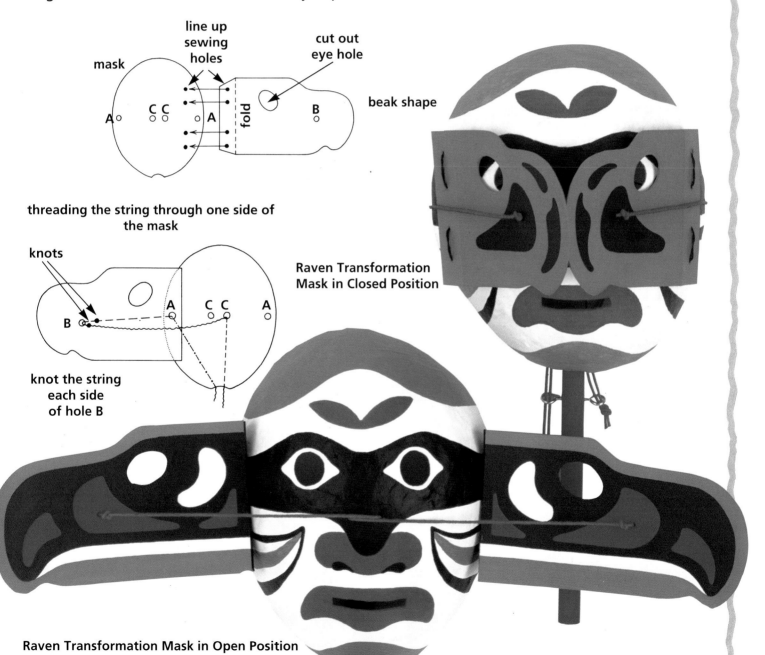

line up sewing holes

cut out eye hole

mask

beak shape

fold

A   C C   A   B

threading the string through one side of the mask

knots

A   C C   A

B

knot the string each side of hole B

Raven Transformation Mask in Closed Position

Raven Transformation Mask in Open Position

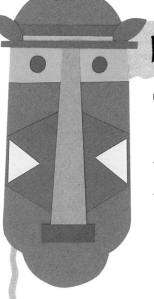

FACES FROM THE PAST

The ancient Egyptians believed that their gods and goddesses took the form of the birds and animals living in the Nile valley. One of the forms of the chief god, Re, was that of a hawk. Thoth the god of wisdom had the head of an ibis and Horus, the sky god, had the head of a falcon. In Mexico, the Mayans and Aztecs had ceremonial masks made of jade. An Aztec mask of cedar wood, turquoise and shell survives today.

Making Mexican Mosaic Masks

1. Find a photograph of a mosaic mask in a book and sketch a design for the mask.

2. Make a papier mâché mask base using the mould method on page 24.

3. Cut eye and nose holes in the mask using a craft knife and paint the mask grey.

4. Copy the pattern lines from the sketch on to the mask base.

5. First work out the mosaic design on the sketch using small pieces of coloured paper. Then glue the pieces on to the mask base following the pattern lines.

6. Attach elastic to the skull to fit round your head. Some Aztec masks had jewellery such as ear rings. You might like to add these to your mask.

Building up the Mosaic Pattern on the Sketch

Aztec Mosaic Mask

Making Egyptian Bird Masks

1. When this mask is worn the base sits on top of the head and is held in place by elastic under the chin. Find pictures of Egyptian gods in reference books to get ideas for your design.

2. Make a papier mâché mask base using the balloon method on page 20. Make sure it is the right size for your head.

3. Cut out the card piece to make the beak as shown.

4. Glue the beak shape to the mask base following the plan shown here. Fold back the tabs and glue the beak to the base.

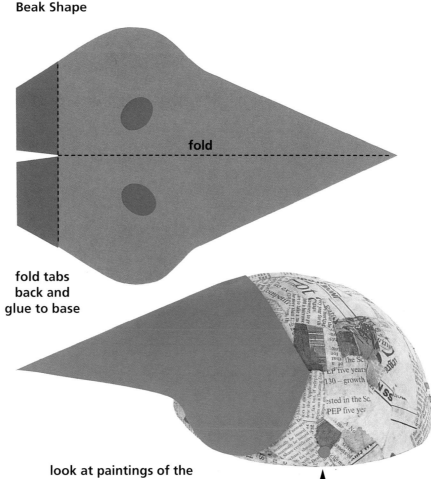

Beak Shape

fold

fold tabs back and glue to base

look at paintings of the Egyptian gods and see the stylised way they were portrayed

make a hole for the elastic

Egyptian Hawk Mask

Painting the Mask Following your Design

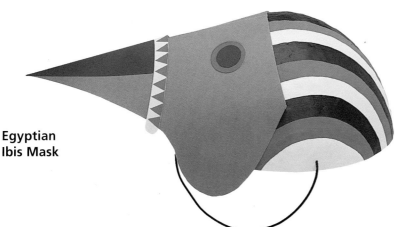

Egyptian Ibis Mask

Tutankhamen

When the tomb of Tutankhamen was first discovered in 1922, the head and shoulders of his mummified body were covered by a beautiful golden mask. He had been dead for more than 3,000 years. The Ancient Egyptians had a very firm belief in an afterlife. The tomb was filled with the things needed for a journey into the next world.

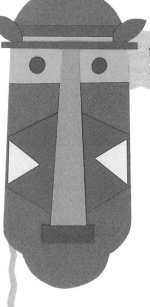

FRIGHTENING FACES

Masks were once worn to summon up good spirits and get rid of evil demons. The Celts celebrated the Feast of Samhain at the end of October and built bonfires to frighten away bad spirits. In Sri Lanka, masks with writhing snakes and bulging eyes made frightening faces. Each of the 18 Sanni devil masks were used to protect against diseases believed to be caused by the devil.

Making a Sand Cast

1. Fill a large plastic bowl (about 45 cm across) with sand that is damp enough to hold its shape.

2. Make a hollow in the sand that is about the size and shape of a head.

3. Draw features in the hollow to form a face. Use different sticks and tools to create the textures.

4. When you are happy with the shape, mix up some plaster to the consistency of thick cream.

5. Pour the plaster slowly into the mould using a spoon to fill in the smaller holes. Try not to disturb the sand.

6. Fill the mould to the top and leave it until the plaster is set.

Tools for Textures

Sand Casting

Sand casting is a good way to make a grotesque mask-like face. However, this mask is really too heavy to be worn.

It can be hung on a wall. You could try copying the faces of goblin, monster and dragon gargoyles that can be seen on some old buildings.

Making the Mould

Cleaning the Cast
Loosen the sand around the plaster and carefully remove the cast from the bowl. Use an old stiff brush to clean all the sand from the plaster face. It will have kept the rough texture of the sand.

Adding the Plaster Carefully to the Mould

Removing the Sand with an Old Brush

Painted, Frightening Face

Decorating the Plaster Mask
1. Paint the plaster face using poster paints. Make the face as frightening as possible.

2. Carefully carve a notch in the back of your cast so you can hang it on the wall.

WORD LIST

ancestors Those from whom others have descended.

anonymous To have kept one's identity secret.

articulated An artefact with joints that make movement possible.

carnival The merrymaking that takes place at festival times. In Roman Catholic countries it is usually before Lent.

comedy Light-hearted and amusing drama.

disguise The concealing of one's identity.

exotic Being strange or unusual.

festival The period of time set aside for a particular celebration. Usually having religious significance.

infamous Having a bad reputation.

inhibitions Feelings that stop some people from having fun.

legend A well-known story, not necessarily true, but passed down from generation to generation.

mime A theatrical performance without words. Meaning is conveyed by gestures and body movements.

phizog Slang for physiognomy. The assessing of character through facial features.

revellers Noisy merrymakers having fun.

reversible Made in such a way that either side can be used.

ritual The traditional pattern or form followed during a ceremony.

rivets Short metal pins for joining sections together.

superstitions Beliefs with no real substance, often relying upon omens and charms.

tragedy A serious drama ending in disaster.

transformation A change in form.

visor A small moveable section designed to protect the face.

vulnerable Exposed to attack.

INDEX